TOUGH JOBS
PIRATE

Helen Greathead

Illustrated by Bob Dewar

A & C Black • London

Welcome to the 18th Century

Imagine a time when:
• Most people never left home ... but some went to sea for years and years.
• People didn't fly in aeroplanes ... they made long journeys in boats with sails.

• People didn't have computers or TVs ... they knew hardly anything about faraway lands.

www.acblack.com

Text copyright © 2007 Helen Grea
Illustrations copyright © 2007 Bob

The rights of Helen Greathead and Bob
be identified as the author and illustrator o
have been asserted by them in accordance
Copyrights, Designs and Patents Act

ISBN 978-0-7136-7775-1 (hbk)
ISBN 978-0-7136-7770-6 (pbk)

A CIP catalogue for this book is availa
from the British Library.

This book is produced using paper that is mad
wood grown in managed, sustainable forests. It i
renewable and recyclable. The logging and manu
processes conform to the environmental regul
of the country of origin.

Printed and bound by MPG Books Ltd, Bodmin,

PIRATE

• Most people went to sea poor, and came back poor, or not at all. But some people did make their fortunes – the ones called pirates.

Pirates have been around for thousands of years, but what is known as "The Golden Age of Piracy" took place 300 years ago. There were more pirates around at that time than at any other, and they plundered the trading ships that sailed on the Caribbean Sea.

The Golden Age didn't last long. The British Government decided to stop Caribbean piracy once and for all. They offered pardons to pirates who gave themselves up, and hangings to those who didn't.

Pirates Ahoy!

Let's pretend you live in the 18th century. Your life in England is being turned upside down, because your dad has a new job – in Jamaica! There's a terrible pirate problem on the Caribbean Sea and he's been sent there to sort it out. Now you and your mum are sailing out to join him.

You left from Plymouth, England, seven weeks ago on a merchant ship. Only one more week to go!

You are the only passengers on the ship. You have a cabin with a bed, and you eat proper dinners at the captain's table. Even so, life at sea is tough. You spend a lot of time on deck, staring at the horizon.

You wish you could chat to the crew, but they never have time. There are only twelve of them, and they are constantly cleaning, doing repairs and sorting out the sails. Captain Shrivel barks orders at them all day long.

One morning, something unusual happens…

"Pirate ship ahoy!" comes a cry from the top of the mainmast.

You look out to sea and spot a ship with a black-and-white flag. Captain Shrivel looks serious. The crew look terrified, your mum looks worried ... but you feel a tingle of excitement.

As the ship moves closer, your mum grabs you. She bundles you down to the ship's hold, right at the bottom of the boat, and pulls out an empty chest.

"Get in," she says.

There's no point in arguing. You climb into the chest, then your mum slams down the lid and locks you inside!

"It's for your own good, son," she says, as she rushes back on deck.

The ship's rats are scrabbling around outside the chest, and the stores stink of filthy water and animal poo! But you push thoughts of seasickness out of your mind and listen hard.

There's a sudden roar of men's voices. Footsteps thunder on the deck above and you hear the *chink, chink* of clashing swords.

Your mum's angry voice rises above the din, but you can't quite hear what she's saying. There's some shouting, then a huge *splash*! Heavy footsteps thump down the steps. You try to spy through the keyhole.

A pair of grubby feet kicks at the storage barrels. Oh no, it must be a pirate! He gets so close you can smell him – phwoar! You tremble as he turns the key. He lifts the lid of the box and you can't help yourself, you lean over the side ... and throw up at his feet.

The pirate has a long scar down his right cheek. He is really old, well over 40! You don't notice the missing fingers at first. You're too busy looking at the tattoos on his arms. Luckily, he isn't angry. In fact, he laughs and yells, "Come and see what Six Fingers has found!"

Thirty or so pirates come running. They laugh at the puddle in front of you.

"Where's my mum?" you shout, darting up the steps.

From the deck you spot her red hair blowing in the wind. The ship's rowing boat is bobbing about in the distance. Captain Shrivel and your ship's crew are on board.

Your mum is waving her arms, shouting, "You scurvy pirates, I'll be back for my boy!"

Mixing with real, live pirates should be a fantastic adventure, but they've set your mum adrift on the high seas. Now the only person left to fight the pirates is you!

The Pirate Ship

There were no planes, trains or cars in the 18th century, so ships were very important.
• Merchant ships carried wool, tea, cloth and other items for sale in far-off countries.
• Navy ships patrolled the high seas and fought battles.

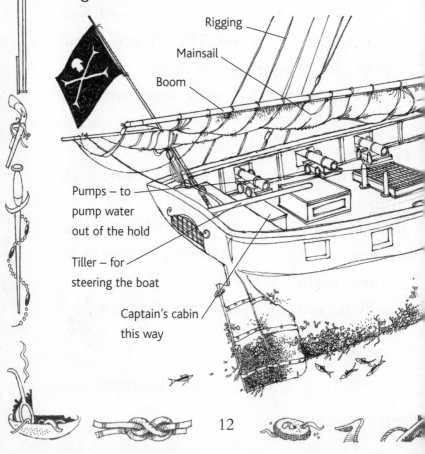

Rigging

Mainsail

Boom

Pumps – to pump water out of the hold

Tiller – for steering the boat

Captain's cabin this way

• Pirate ships carried a rabble of thieving pirates, who attacked and robbed all the other ships!

This boat is a sloop. Sloops were used as merchant ships, but pirates liked them, too. They were small and fast, so they were ideal for making a quick getaway.

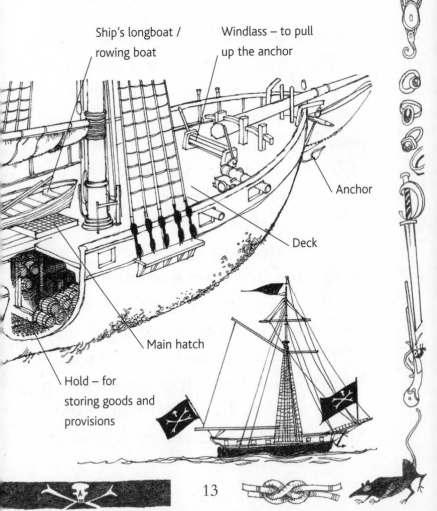

Ship's longboat / rowing boat

Windlass – to pull up the anchor

Anchor

Deck

Main hatch

Hold – for storing goods and provisions

A Pirate's Mate

You stare after the boat as it disappears.

"The captain won't have a woman on his ship. Says they always bring bad luck," says Six Fingers. "He likes young boys even less." Then, seeing your look of horror, he adds, "Best stick with me, lad, and you'll be all right."

That sounds like a good plan. If Six Fingers wasn't slashing open every barrel on the ship, he'd seem quite nice. Maybe you won't fight the pirates after all. Instead, you could try being friendly.

"There's no treasure here," you tell Six Fingers, as you follow him about the ship.

Two men are struggling to lift a canon. And the pirate's carpenter is drawing circles on the side of the boat. Six Fingers ignores them. He climbs down the ladder and marches straight into the captain's cabin, without even knocking! You go with him.

Six Fingers runs his hands over the navigating tools. "No treasure you say?" he smiles. "But here's a fine brass compass. We need equipment like this."

"Then come this way!" you squeak.
You show Six Fingers a chest in the
corner of the cabin.
Inside, are little bottles
filled with powders
and potions. You
stand back, feeling
pleased with yourself.

"Where's Six Fingers Sam the
Quartermaster?" a voice booms from
outside.

"In here, Cap'n
Flogg," Six Fingers
replies.

"Any good spoils?"
the captain bellows.

"Aye, sir. Here's
that medical chest
you was wanting."

The captain strides into the cabin,
"Well found," he says, patting Six Fingers
on the shoulder.

Wow! Although his clothes are grubby and his skin all tanned and wrinkly, the captain is a fashionable man. He wears a wig of real hair, a fine silk cravat, and a very fancy coat. His shoes even have smart, red heels.

You hope Six Fingers will tell the captain how he found the medical chest. But the captain scowls when he sees you.

"Huh, heard there was a boy on board," he sneers as he looks you up and down. "Well, don't stand there idling, lad, you're a pirate now."

"Yes, sir," you say, eagerly.

"Find a cloth and clean up that mess you made," the captain barks. "Then go out and swab the deck. It's time you got those fine clothes dirty."

Up on deck, you see a shabby-looking pirate ship moored alongside yours. The pirates are shifting food, drink, gunpowder, weapons and even animals across from one ship to the other.

Six Fingers appears with a bucket of vinegar and water.

You dip in your cloth and start scrubbing, but you can't help staring at the pirates. Six Fingers tells you who's who.

"Emmanuel there, he's our cook. He was an African slave, but escaped the sugar plantations in Jamaica." He points to a boy who doesn't look a lot older than you.

"Juan is our boatswain, learned the ropes on a Spanish treasure ship. His mate, Hans, is from Holland. He's the master gunner. Most of us are English, Welsh and Scots. Everyone's welcome here, as long as they work hard and stick to the rules."

You can't help noticing that lots of the pirates have big, scabby spots on their faces.

"We can't always eat as we should," Six Fingers explains. "Disease and infections are easy to catch. They kill pirates and sailors alike."

The pirates dress just like other seamen you've seen, except they're scruffier and they don't have shoes – but they do wear jewellery!

"Bring on the rum, lads," shouts Juan.

You suddenly realise the pirates aren't taking stuff off the ship, they are bringing things on board. Now you see their plan. They're leaving their old boat behind – and making your boat their new home!

Tough Jobs for Pirates

Pirates often stole the merchant ships they attacked. Sometimes they even stole the crew! Merchant sailors worked hard for little food and hardly any pay. Pirates shared everything between them and life was often easier with more men to do the work, so merchant sailors were happy to join them. But a pirate ship had lots of mouths to feed ... and there was more competition for the top jobs:

Captain – men do what the captain tells them in battle, but if they don't like his style, they can vote him out.

Quartermaster – shares out the 'booty' (that's any money made from pirate raids). He shares out punishments, too!

The Sailing Master – works out the route and decides how to set the sails.

Boatswain (bosun) – makes sure the ship is fit to sail.

Master Gunner – is in charge of the gun crew and all their weapons.

Carpenter – can repair the ship ... and chop off the leg of a wounded pirate.

Cook – ideal job for a wounded pirate – even if he can't cook.

Musician – entertains the pirates at night – and keeps a steady beat when the pirates are attacking.

Party Time

You've been a pirate for three whole days, and you've never worked so hard in your life. Whilst other pirates take turns to work, the captain won't let you rest. Your smart clothes are getting shabby. There are holes in your white stockings, and your coat is covered in dirt.

You're not allowed to sleep in your cabin any more. Instead, you sleep on deck with most of the other men. Some have lumpy mattresses, but you have a hammock. When you finally manage to climb in, you find it's quite comfy, but you don't sleep well. You're thinking about what Captain Flogg will make you do tomorrow.

In the morning, you try to sneak back to your old cabin for a sleep – but you can't find it! The ship's carpenter has knocked it down.

"I'm opening up the ship," he tells you, cheerily, "to make more room for fighting."

"You won't survive a battle dressed like that," scoffs Juan, joining you. "Want to look like a real pirate?"

"Ooh, er, yes," you answer.

"Shoes and stockings off," says Juan. Then he takes your coat and slices off the sleeves with his cutlass! The carpenter wraps a red scarf round your head.

Six Fingers appears with a bucket of black paint. "Off with yer breeches," he commands.

You're not sure about giving up your trousers, but Six Fingers grabs them anyway – and splatters them with paint!

"Slip 'em back on when they're dry," says Six Fingers. "The black tar will protect against the rain. Can stop a sword slash, too. We'll find you a jewel on the next ship we raid!"

You can't help feeling proud, but you're still hopping about in your underwear when there's a shout from the quarterdeck.

"We've worked hard!" Captain Flogg bellows. "She's a fine ship with good supplies. All those for celebrating, say aye."

The answer is a deafening "AYE".

"Break open the rum. There are rations for all. We'll take turns on watch," says Captain Flogg. "The young lad can go and help Cook."

"A toast to all pirates," someone shouts, holding up a rum-filled tankard.

"To all pirates," the crew chorus.

The ship doesn't have a proper kitchen, just a huge pot hanging over a bricked-in fire.

Emmanuel laughs when he sees your underwear. "Getting ready for the pot, lad?" he grins. "Nothing would surprise me with Captain Flogg in charge!"

The pot is enormous – you'd easily fit inside! Luckily, Emmanuel already has some eggs from the ship's hens. He's skinned a ship's goat, for cooking, too.

You are soon chopping onions, cabbage and pickled fish. Emmanuel throws them all into the pot. He adds olives, grapes, spices – and some funny-looking fruit. It smells so much better than the salt meat and biscuits you've been eating since the pirates claimed the ship.

"Try some Salmagundi stew," says Emmanuel, handing you a biscuit for dipping.

It tastes delicious – but you spot something moving about in the biscuit. Eurgh – a weevil!

Emmanuel laughs. "Take my advice," he snorts, "only eat hard tack biscuits after dark."

Up on deck, as the evening wears on, some men have a game of cards, roll dice or sing sea shanties as the fiddle and accordion play.

Your trousers are dry at last. You slip them back on and try to sit down. They're so stiff that you can hardly bend.

It's time to change over the watch, but some pirates are sprawled face-down on the deck. Three dancing men topple over as a big wave hits the ship. And Six Fingers pulls two quarrelling pirates apart. "Remember the rules, lads," he warns. "No fighting on the ship."

You wonder which rules he is talking about.

The winds are picking up, and the waves are getting stronger! There's a storm brewing, and half the crew are drunk! A sudden wave sends you rolling across the deck. Captain Flogg spots you sprawled on the floor – and laughs.

Pirate Rules

Pirates knew from experience some of the terrible things that could happen at sea. Before a pirate ship sailed, they all agreed a set of rules they would live by. The rules, or "ship's articles", made sure life would be better for pirates than it was for ordinary sailors. Every pirate had to swear to stick to them:

• All pirates vote on big decisions.
• Every pirate has a right to fresh food and drink (no favours for the captain!).
• Every seaman gets one share of any booty. The captain gets two shares. Other pirates with top jobs get one and a half. Boys only get a half share.
• If you steal from another pirate you will be marooned.

- Lights out at eight o'clock.
- Everyone keeps their own weapons fit for fighting.
- No women on board – it can only bring bad luck.

- No fighting on board – quarrels are to be settled on land with swords and pistols.
- If you lose an arm, a leg or an eye in battle, you get extra money to make up for it.

- The first pirate to spot another ship gets to use the best pistol.

All Hands on Deck

Captain Flogg lowers his stubbly face so it's level with yours. "Right," he orders. "Up the rigging with you!"

You start climbing the rope ladders that stretch to the top of the masts. You are soaking wet and freezing cold. The winds are getting stronger all the time. Why is Captain Flogg always so horrible to you? You could fall off and…

"Keep looking up, mate," calls Juan as he rushes up behind you. "You're no good to us down in Davy Jones' locker!"

Thank goodness you're not alone!

As the wind crashes into the ship, you cling to the ropes. Your legs are like jelly, but you manage to wrap them around the ladder as you roll down the sail. You glimpse the chaos on deck as you struggle back down. More men are on hand now, and they are pulling out covers to stop water pouring into the hatches.

"Watch out for the guns," shouts Juan. "If one slips from its place it can crush you flat."

You're hardly able to stand when you reach the deck, but there's still so much to do. Men are tying the guns to the sides. Boxes, chicken coops and drunken pirates are sliding about everywhere. A huge crate is about to topple overboard. You run to stop it. The captain gets there first … and pushes it over the side!

"Boat's too low in the water. Got to lighten her load," barks Captain Flogg. "Throw anything you can into the sea!"

Suddenly, there's a huge wave. The ship rolls sideways and men fly across the deck. Water is pouring in.

"Man the pumps!" yells Six Fingers.

Some of the sozzled pirates head down below to pump out the water.

Finally, the wind starts to drop. The storm has passed, but the sails are ripped and there's damage to the mast. Still, you and the ship have survived and, as the sun comes up and the cloud clears, you can see land!

It's a small island the pirates seem to know. It has a fabulous, golden beach. Some of the pirates dive straight into the sparkly, blue-green water, and splash around fully dressed.

"Go on, jump in," says Juan.

"Can't swim," you hiss, hoping no one else will hear. But Juan just laughs and throws you overboard! You're convinced you're going to drown, then Hans catches you – phew!

You spend the next hour splashing around in the water. Juan gives you a swimming lesson, holding you up by your breeches. You stick your face into the water. It's fantastic! There are fish of all different colours and sizes – and strange, round creatures nearly as big as you are!

"Turtles," shouts Juan, as he pulls you along.

"We'll take one onto the ship later," adds Hans.

Great, you think. Loads of pirates have pets – monkeys, cats, even a parrot. Yours will be the best!

Later, Hans and Juan are getting ready to row to the island to look for food.

"Can I come?" you ask, eagerly.

"Why not," says Juan. "We can teach you to hunt."

But Captain Flogg spoils things, as usual. "No you don't," he says, dragging you off, "there's work to be done."

First, the ship has to be hauled out of the water, using ropes and pulleys, then the carpenter and his team push it over!

"It has to be careened," explains Six Fingers. "You can help me scrape barnacles and weeds off the ship's bottom. They slow the ship down, see?"

You do your best, but you mainly scrape skin off your fingers.

Some men are fixing rotten planks, while the carpenter cuts holes in the sides of the ship for the extra guns.

Next day, there are more repairs. The first job is to bind together the ropes that snapped in the storm. Then it's sail fixing. You've got a leather strap to protect your hand, but the sailcloth is tough. Your hand aches and you stop work for a moment.

Captain Flogg is furious, "I'll have you keelhauled!" he shouts.

You show him your blistered hands and, grumpily, he lets you rest.

After a few days, the boat is afloat again. Hans helps you heave your turtle friend onto the deck. You carry it down to the bilge. There's water down there – it's rotten and stinking, but he should feel more at home.

"What happens now?" you ask Six Fingers, sleepily, over supper.

"We'll set off and find a ship to raid. We lost so much in the storm. We got fruits and birds from the island, but we've no more salt meat."

"So what are we eating then?" You stop chewing and look at your plate. The stew has gristly, green lumps in it.

"Turtle," says Six Fingers, with a grin on his face. "Tasty, ain't it?"

41

Pirate Talk

To be a good pirate, you'll need to learn the language:

You don't become a pirate, you **go on the account**.

Want everyone to stop what they're doing? Then say, "**Avast ye!**"

Need help on deck? Shout, "**All hands hoay!**"

Need a pee? Head for the **heads**.

Don't eat eggs. Eat **cackle fruit**.

A friendly pirate might **give quarter** – or show mercy.

A nasty pirate **gives no quarter**!

Stay away from **scurvy pirates**. Scurvy is a deadly disease caused by lack of fruit.

If a pirate calls you a **landlubber**, he thinks you're a rotten pirate.

If he calls you a **hornswaggler**, he thinks you're a cheat.

And if he threatens to **keelhaul** you, run for it! He wants to tie you to a rope and drop you in the sea. Then he'll pull you under the ship and back up the other side!

If a pirate is caught, he isn't hanged, he **dances the hempen jig**.

And anyway, pirates don't die, they just **visit Davy Jones' locker**.

Attack!

When Hans finds out about the turtle, he assures you that there are others on board. As soon as you can, you rush down to the hold and find *your* turtle, safe and well.

While you're there, you spot Captain Flogg and Six Fingers bending over a chest full of flags! There are black-and-white pirate flags, black-and-red pirate flags and multi-coloured flags from all over the world.

"This'll do," says Captain Flogg, snatching a British flag. He grabs you, as you pass. "Come with me, boy," he says. "Here, get dressed."

In the middle of the captain's cabin are your clothes, clean and ready to wear.

"But I thought I had to dress like a pirate?" you argue.

"Come on, we haven't got all day," says Captain Flogg, stamping about the cabin.

But he isn't talking to you. Juan walks out from behind a screen. He's wearing one of your mum's dresses! His face is bright red. You'd be angry, if he didn't look so stupid.

At last Captain Flogg explains what's going on. "There's a merchant ship on the horizon," he says. "We're going to pretend to be friendly, sail up slowly … then attack!

"We'll be disguised as an English ship," Captain Flogg continues. "You and Juan will walk the deck like normal passengers, while the crew hides below!"

Up on deck, it's spookily quiet. Men everywhere are polishing their weapons and checking their guns. Hans runs the new flag up the flagpole.

Six Fingers is pouring sand on the deck. "It's to soak up blood after the fight," he whispers.

Others are drenching blankets in water, "just in case there's a fire".

You start to worry. "Can I have a weapon?" you ask.

"Certainly not," says Six Fingers, firmly. "You wouldn't want to end up with a wooden leg at your age!

"Anyway," he adds, "if it gets rough, the captain wants you to fetch the gunpowder from down below."

"Why don't they keep the gunpowder by the guns?" you ask.

Six Fingers roars with laughter. "What, and let one stray spark from a pistol blow the whole ship sky high?"

Captain Flogg orders the ship to slow down. You and Juan stroll the deck, arm in arm. As the two ships come close, pirates crouch down behind the rails. Others hide below deck. Only a small group of men will board the ship. Everyone else has to stay put until they're told to move.

The merchant ship pulls alongside you. The crew shouts a friendly greeting, but the pirates answer with a racket of shouting, jeering and – oo-er – swear words you've never even *heard* before.

Juan whips off his dress. He and Six Fingers throw grappling hooks across to the other ship. The hooks pull the boats together, so it's easy to hop across.

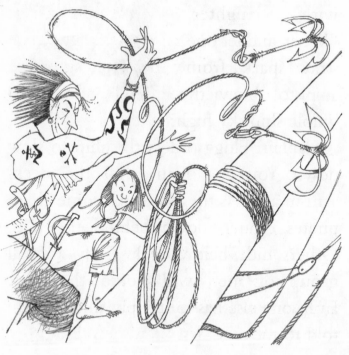

Some pirates wave their weapons in the air. Others fire their pistols or hurl smoking hand grenades onto the other boat. You hear canon blasts from the gun deck below.

"If they resist, show no quarter," yells Captain Flogg.

You brace yourself for the fight, but it's all over in minutes! Six Fingers and a group of pirates leap onto the merchant ship. Captain Flogg talks to the crew. The next thing you know, they've all agreed to come "on the account". They all want to be pirates! You feel slightly disappointed, but at least you've still got both legs.

The other ship is loaded with gunpowder, salt meat and rope. There are good sails, and a few barrels of rum. And Six Fingers presses something into your hand and winks. It is a golden medallion. Your first pirate jewel!

Pirate Tactics

As a pirate, carrying loads of weapons makes you look really mean:

Hand grenade – fill it with gunpowder, light the fuse and hurl it at the enemy ship.

Flintlock pistols – tied with ribbon so you can dangle them round your neck.

Dagger

Cutlass – its short blade won't get caught in the rigging.

Boarding axe – for boarding ship and cutting ropes.

Grappling hook – helps pull other boats towards yours.

You can make your boat look nasty too:

• A red pirate flag means you will give no quarter.
• A Jolly Roger means you will give quarter – as long as everyone does as you say!

• Guns make the ship look scarier, but it takes six men to load each canon, light the fuse and fire it.

If pirates want to take over a ship, they'll be careful not to damage it with cannon balls. Damaging people isn't such a problem. Pirates like to fight face to face. But, if a crew is scared silly before the attack, they'll give themselves up sooner. Then the pirates don't need to bother fighting at all!

Maiden's Revenge

Weeks later, you're sunning yourself on deck munching on a juicy mango. Life is much easier since the new crew came on the account. Captain Flogg has different people to order about.

Suddenly, you hear someone shouting, "Ship ahoy!" A small ship is heading straight towards you – and it's flying a pirate flag!

"She's called the *Maiden's Revenge*," says Captain Flogg, looking through his telescope.

Why does she want revenge, you wonder?

"Gunner, have your crew on standby," orders Captain Flogg. "Hold fire unless I give the signal."

The ships draw near, and both captains eye each other suspiciously. The captain of the *Maiden's Revenge* is a tall man. Next to him stands a small pirate, wearing a red headscarf and hat.

"Captain Flogg?" asks the tall captain.
"Aye," says Captain Flogg. "And you?"
"Captain Heller," he replies.

You don't catch what they say next, but soon Heller is climbing aboard. The small pirate comes, too. There's something strangely familiar about him.

You follow them down to the captain's  cabin, and listen outside the door.

You can just hear them saying things like "Two's company" and "There's safety in numbers".

It sounds like they're plotting to sail together. With two ships it's easier to attack, and you can share supplies.

You nip to the "heads". The sea is quite choppy. Waves that clean away the mess under the toilets give your bottom a good wash too. Then, just as you finish, the small pirate comes marching in.

"Ah, there you are," he says.

Your face turns scarlet. What does he want with you?

"It's all right," he says. "I've seen it all before." The boy takes off his hat and scarf. Long curls of red hair tumble out. He really has seen it all before. He's your mum!

"Don't worry," your mum whispers. She tucks her hair under her scarf, "Everything's under control. Just pretend you don't know me."

You want to ask all sorts of questions, but there's no time. Your mum is already heading back on deck. What is she up to?

The two ships set sail for a bay Heller knows. You're on board with just a handful of pirates, when you hear a funny, scrabbling noise.

A hand comes over the side of the boat. A body follows it over. It's a man, wearing a bright-red jacket and white breeches. A naval officer!

A stream of sailors swarms onto the deck after him.

You're just trying to decide what to do, when one of them grabs you and covers your mouth with his hand.

The men drag you along to the captain's cabin and push you into the middle of the room. Now you see Captain Heller properly for the first time.

"Dad!" you yell, and the game is up.

Your mum throws herself on top of you, and your dad grabs his pistol. There's a clink of cutlasses, and a couple of gunshots.

Your mum is shouting for everyone to stop and they do – once Captain Flogg, Six Fingers, Juan and Hans have been rounded up. They look really miserable.

It's brilliant to see your parents again, but what will happen to your shipmates?

You've never seen your dad so serious. "Piracy is a terrible crime," he tells Captain Flogg. "You've terrorised the seas for far too long. You show no mercy, and I shall show no mercy to you. I'll see you lot hang."

"No!" you hear yourself shout. "They're my friends. They didn't hurt me and I've learned so much. And didn't you say there were new ways to deal with pirates?"

Your dad looks cross and flustered. He clears his throat. "I suppose there is another way – give up being pirates. Fight piracy with us instead and there will be no … further … punishment."

The pirates mutter gruff thanks under their breath.

"And you can stop *playing* pirates, too, my boy!" Dad glares at you. "In a few years' time, you'll be hunting down these villains with me!"

"What a waste," Six Fingers mutters under his breath. "The boy makes a really fine pirate."

"Aye," Captain Flogg agrees. "Being a pirate is a tough job. Not everyone can do it. But this boy could be one of the best."

It's the nicest thing you've ever heard Captain Flogg say, and it starts you thinking. Maybe one day you *will* go to sea again. Maybe you'll even captain your own ship! But, you promise yourself, whichever type of ship you sail, you'll be a good captain, fair to all men – and turtles, too.

Famous Pirates - Three of the Best

Most of the Golden Age pirates are long forgotten, but some names are still famous today.

Edward Teach, or **Blackbeard**, was famous because:

- He was the cruellest pirate ever
- He tied black ribbons in his bushy black beard
- He pushed lighted ropes under his hat so he'd look more scary
- He was hunted down and killed by a Naval Lieutenant
- His head was hung at the front of his ship as a warning to other pirates
- But nobody EVER found his treasure!

Anne Bonny was famous because:

- She was a woman
- Her mum dressed her as a boy when was young
- She carried on dressing as a man to earn a living
- She sailed with another woman – Mary Read
- She was sentenced to death and survived, because she was pregnant
- But then she disappeared, and was never seen again.

Bartholomew Roberts, or **Black Bart**, was famous because:

- He preferred drinking tea to rum
- He liked to wear fine clothes
- He commanded four ships, and over 500 men
- He plundered and sank 400 ships
- He was a pirate for around four short years
- He was killed when the navy finally found him
- But he was probably the most successful pirate EVER.

Glossary

articles – the rules that pirates drew up among themselves and agreed to live by

barnacle – small creature with hard shell that sticks to the bottom of a ship

booty – the things pirates take from other ships and divide up between them

breeches – short trousers, fastened below the knee

careen – to turn a ship on its side and clean and mend it

century – a hundred-year time period

compass – an instrument used to find direction

cravat – a strip of fabric worn around the neck

gunpowder – an explosive powder used to fire guns and cannon

hanging – method of killing convicted pirates by dangling them by a rope tied round the neck

heads – the ship's toilets

horizon – the line where the sea and sky appear to meet

lieutenant – an officer who is second in command

marooned – punishment where someone is put ashore with a pistol that has one shot and a day's supply of water

medallion – large medal that hangs around the neck

merchant – a person who buys and sells things to make money

naval – connected with the navy

pardon – to be forgiven by the authorities

plunder – to take someone else's property violently

rigging – ropes that hold a ship's sails

sea shanty – song a sailor sings

sailcloth – material used to make and mend sails

salt meat – meat that has been preserved using salt

scurvy – a disease common among sailors caused by lack of vitamin C

swab – to clean, using a mop or cloth

tar – a sticky, black liquid that was used to protect wood

telescope – an instrument used to make distant objects appear closer

toast – to drink good health to a person or thing

WITH SO MANY **TOUGH JOB** TO CHOOSE FROM...

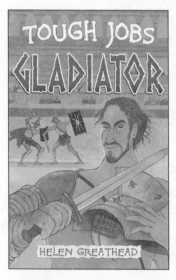

WHICH ONE WILL **YOU** TRY NEXT?